DISCOVERING
ANCIENT CIVILIZATIONS

THE AZTECS

David West

I0808440

Gareth Stevens
PUBLISHING

Please visit our website, www.garethstevens.com.
For a free color catalog of all our high-quality books,
call toll free 1-800-542-2595 or fax 1-877-542-2596.

Cataloging-in-Publication Data

Names: West, David.
Title: The Aztecs / David West.
Description: New York : Gareth Stevens Publishing, 2017. | Series: Discovering ancient civilizations | Includes index.
Identifiers: ISBN 9781482450552 (pbk.) | ISBN 9781482450576 (library bound) | ISBN 9781482450569 (6 pack)
Subjects: LCSH: Aztecs–Juvenile literature. | Indians of Mexico–Juvenile literature.
Classification: LCC F1219.73 W47 2017 | DDC 972'.018–dc23

First Edition

Published in 2017 by
Gareth Stevens Publishing
111 East 14th Street, Suite 349
New York, NY 10003

Designed by David West Books

Printed in the United States of America
CPSIA compliance information: Batch #CS16GS: For further information contact Gareth Stevens, New York, New York at 1-800-542-2595.

DISCOVERING
ANCIENT CIVILIZATIONS

THE AZTECS

David West

Gareth Stevens
PUBLISHING

CONTENTS

The Aztecs Ruled an Empire

Aztecs were the people known as Mexica, who settled in the valley of Mexico. Their capital city was Tenochtitlán. Aztecs may also include the Acolhuas of Texcoco and the Tepanecs of Tlacopan who, together with the Mexica, formed the Aztec Triple Alliance which controlled the "Aztec empire."

The Aztec empire was ruled from Tenochtitlán by the emperor who expected tributes to be paid to him by the conquered city-states. Tributes were paid two to four times a year. They included luxury items like feathers, greenstone beads, and adorned suits, and goods such as cloth, firewood, and food.

The Aztec population was made up of royalty, nobles, merchants, commoners, and slaves.

The map shows the Aztec empire in red. The inset map shows the five lakes and the Triple Alliance cities in bold.

Aztecs Built Farms on Water

Lake Texcoco, in the valley of Mexico, surrounded Tenochtitlán. Land around the edges of the city and other shallow parts of the lake was reclaimed by creating artificial islands. These "chinampa" provided extra areas to grow food and did not need to rely on rain. They were easily watered from the lake and had up to seven harvests a year.

Farmers on a chinampa load up a canoe with food to be given in tribute to the noble who owned it. The rest will be eaten or sold at the market.

Among the crops grown on chinampas were maize (corn), beans, squash, avocados, tomatoes, chili peppers, and flowers. They also used cotton plants to make clothing. Maize could be stored for a long time and ground into flour.

The Aztecs also made popcorn from maize.

AZTECS USED CHOCOLATE AS MONEY

The market played an important role in Aztec life. People would meet there and swap news and gossip. Apart from food the market offered various goods from raw materials to finished products. Jewelry, feathers, animal hides, cloth, **obsidian** blades, baskets, medicine, and even slaves were just a few of the things available.

*At a market people catch up on the latest gossip as others **barter** for goods such as food, pots, firewood, and clothing.*

Certain products had a specific value and could be used like money. Cocoa beans were used as small change. Thirty beans bought a rabbit. For expensive items, lengths of cloth, copper ax blades, or quills full of gold dust were used.

Dishonest people were known to fake cocoa beans by making copies in wax or dough.

AZTECS LOVED ARTS AND CRAFTS

Artists and craftworkers were highly regarded by the Aztecs. They held a good social position in Aztec society, just below the merchants. Aztec craftworkers made luxury items, such as clothing and shields, from brightly colored feathers. Others made masks and jewelry from **jade** and **turquoise** and other precious stones.

A woman weaves a brightly colored cloak on a loom while others work with feathers and clay.

Smiths fashioned intricate ear and nose plugs from gold and silver. The pottery-making center of Cholula produced highly decorated pieces to sell to the wealthy.

*Artists produced sculptures, such as this "**Sun Stone**," and paintings of religious subjects that decorated their temples.*

Merchants acted as spies

Merchants that traveled long distances to trade with various peoples in the Aztec empire and beyond were called pochteca. As well as obtaining goods from distant places they traded surplus goods that the Aztec nobles had received in tribute. The pochteca were very wealthy and occupied a status just below the nobles in Aztec society.

A merchant and his porters leave Tenochtitlán along a causeway as the sun sets. Woven cloth and cocoa pods are carried to barter with.

Although they were powerful the pochteca avoided attracting attention and wore plain clothing in public. Many were spies, reporting on places they visited.

Being a pochteca could be dangerous. If they were suspected of spying in enemy territories they were put to death.

CHILDREN WORKED FROM FOUR YEARS OLD

Children were regarded as **divine** gifts by their parents. Party celebrations at the birth of a child lasted for four days. From the age of four children were expected to do simple chores like fetching water and wood, and sweeping up. They were taught good manners such as eating and drinking slowly. They had to wash after eating, and pick up any leftovers.

The mother of a typical Aztec family prepares the main meal of the day. Children are given chores to do by their father.

Aztec children were brought up to be good examples of what the community expected them to be and do. They were continually lectured by their parents about their gods and how to behave in society.

Being lazy or disobedient was punished severely. Children might be held over a smoking fire of chiles.

AZTEC CHILDREN WENT TO SCHOOL

All Aztec children began full-time education at the age of 15. There were two types of schools. **Calmecac**, a kind of religious academy, was mainly for the children of nobles. Here they were trained to be priests and studied astronomy, writing, calendars, math, medicine, law, and religion. Trainee priests also had to do farmwork, gather firewood, and prepare meals.

Boys at a telpochcalli practice fighting with ***macuahuitls*** *with the obsidian blades removed.*

Telpochcalli was for the children of commoners. Boys had military training and lessons in history and religion. Girls learned craft skills, like embroidery and weaving.

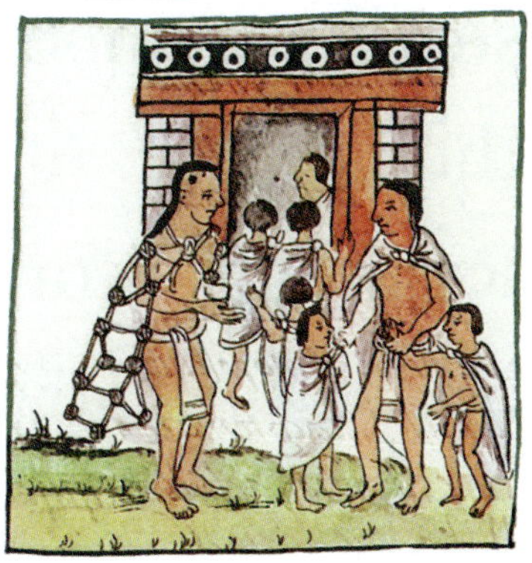

In the early evening children at the Telpochcalli met at the ***cuicacalli*** *to learn and play music, as well as to sing, dance, and get to know each other.*

Warriors Wore Feathered Battle Dress

Aztec armies were made up of large numbers of commoners who had limited training, and a smaller number of professional warriors who belonged to the nobility. A warrior's appearance showed his rank. Rank was awarded according to a warrior's success in battle, and how many enemy soldiers he captured. Captured warriors were taken back to be sacrificed.

Aztec warriors of various ranks dressed in colorful, feathered outfits. The jaguar and eagle costumes were worn by higher ranks.

Aztec warriors carried obsidian-bladed weapons and shields made of wicker, which were covered with colorful designs made from feathers.

A section from a ***codex*** *shows the promotion of a warrior priest from a one-capture rank (top left) to a more than four-captures rank, denoted by the jaguar outfit (bottom right).*

20,000 PEOPLE WERE SACRIFICED EACH YEAR

The Aztecs worshiped many gods. They believed the gods required human blood to keep the world from disaster. Both young and old people were sacrificed, and in different ways, depending on which god they were sacrificed to. Many required the heart to be wrenched from the victim's chest while it was still beating. As many as 2,000 could be sacrificed in a day.

A priest holds up a heart as its owner is thrown down the steps of the pyramid. A second captive is held in place, ready to be sacrificed.

Most victims were willing to be sacrificed. They believed it was a great honor to be selected. In some cases the victim's body was cut up and cooked to be eaten at a festival.

Most human sacrifices were held in front of temples, on top of step pyramids in Tenochtitlán.

SOME WARRIORS FOUGHT WITH FEATHERS

On certain occasions warriors captured in war were taken to a large sacrificial stone in front of the great temple at Tenochtitlán. Here they were given a weapon, such as a macuahuitl, which had feathers instead of obsidian blades. Eagle and jaguar warriors, with obsidian-bladed weapons, took turns to fight the captive.

A captured warrior, with a feathered weapon, fights eagle and jaguar warriors on a sacrificial stone in a ritual combat.

Tlahuicol, a captured Tlaxcalan captain, was forced to fight in the ritual. He succeeded in killing eight jaguar and eagle warriors. He was offered a place in the Aztec army but refused, preferring to be sacrificed.

Captive warriors were tied to the sacrificial stone at the temple.

AZTECS LIKED TO PLAY BALL

The Aztec ball game, ullamaliztli, was played on an "I"-shaped court with a stone hoop in the middle of each long wall. The ball was made of rubber and the two opposing teams had to get the ball through the hoop. The ball had to be kept in the air. The players were not allowed to use their hands or feet. Only the elbows, knees, hips, and head were used.

Spectators look down on the ullamaliztli players in the ball court as the two opposing teams try to get the rubber ball through the stone hoop.

During the game, gambling was common among the spectators. Just about anything could be gambled, from feathers and land to children, and even themselves.

The game had ritual significance and represented the struggle between day and night. Often the winners had the privilege of being sacrificed!

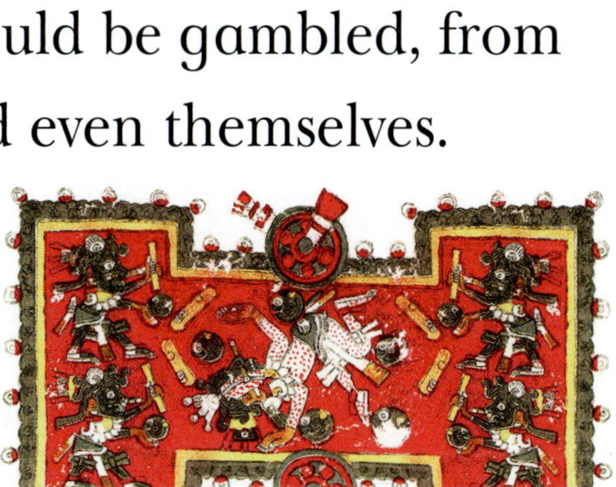

THE AZTEC EMPIRE WAS DESTROYED IN 1521

In March, 1519, a small force of Spanish **conquistadors,** led by **Hernán Cortés,** landed at Veracruz. By November, Cortés and his army were in the Aztec capital as guests of the emperor, Montezuma. The people soon tired of Cortés's men's lust for gold and their religion. In June 1520, the Spanish fled as the Aztecs revolted and killed Montezuma.

Spanish conquistadors and their Tlaxcalan allies battle with Aztec warriors before the great pyramid in Tenochtitlán.

Cortés made an alliance with the **Tlaxcalans** and returned to Tenochtitlán in 1521. The Aztecs, weak from an epidemic of **smallpox**, were defeated by mid-August. The Aztec empire never recovered.

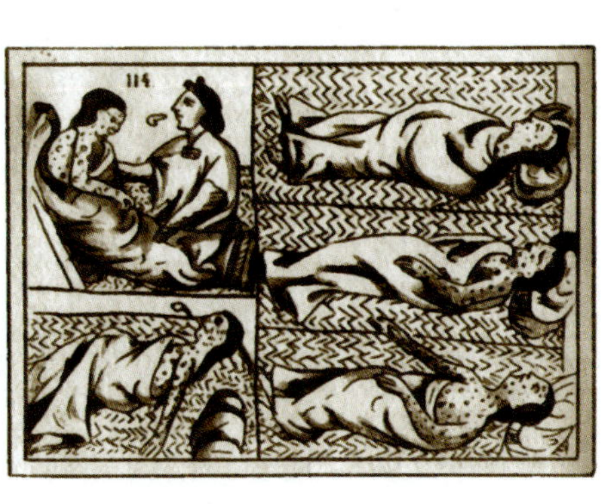

Millions of Aztecs died from smallpox, a disease brought by the invading Spanish.

GLOSSARY

barter
Exchange goods or services for other goods or services without using money.

calmecac
"The house of lineage," the school for the children of Aztec nobility.

codex
A book of pictograms where the sheets of paper were often folded like an accordion.

conquistadors
Soldiers or explorers of the Spanish and Portuguese empires during the Age of Discovery. They conquered and colonized territories in the Americas, Oceania, Africa, and Asia and opened up trade routes.

cuicacalli
"The house of song," a building near the palace in Tenochtitlán where groups of noble warriors gathered to practice dances and songs. It was also where the children of the commoners were trained in music.

divine
Of the gods or god.

Hernán Cortés
A Spanish conquistador who led the expedition that caused the fall of the Aztec empire in 1521. Born in Medellin, Spain, in 1485 he pursued a life of adventure in the New World, leaving for Hispaniola in 1504. He returned to Spain in 1541 where he died six years later.

jade
A green rock, highly prized by the Aztecs, which was carved to make ornaments.

macuahuitl
A wooden sword with obsidian blades used by Aztec warriors.

obsidian
A naturally occurring volcanic glass which fractures easily, creating very sharp splinters which were used by the Aztecs as blades for their weapons.

smallpox
An infectious disease that killed around thirty-five percent of those that contracted it. It was unknown in the Americas until 1520 when the conquistadors arrived in Mexico, bringing the disease with them.

Sun Stone
Also known as the Aztec calendar stone, it is a famous work of Aztec sculpture. It is covered in carvings that some experts think represent a calendar.

telpochcalli
"The house of the young men," the school for the children of commoners.

Tlaxcalans
The group of people that lived in the republic of Tlaxcala that was never conquered by the Aztec Triple Alliance. The Spanish conquistadors formed an alliance with them to defeat the Aztecs.

turquoise
A blue-green gemstone used to make jewelry.

INDEX

FOR MORE INFORMATION

BOOKS

DK Publishing. *DK Eyewitness Books: Aztec, Inca & Maya.* London: Penguin, 2011.

Ollhoff, Jim. *Mayan and Aztec Mythology.* Minneapolis: ABDO, 2011.

WEBSITES

The Awesome Aztecs
aztecs.mrdonn.org/

Ducksters – Aztecs, Maya, Inca
www.ducksters.com/history/aztec_maya_inca.php